AF700698

The Missions: California's Heritage

MISSION NUESTRA SEÑORA de LA SOLEDAD

by

Mary Null Boulé

PROPERTY OF
ANAHEIM PUBLIC LIBRARY
500 WEST BROADWAY
ANAHEIM, CALIFORNIA 92805
EAST HILLS

Merryant Publishers, Inc.
Vashon, WA 98070
206-463-3879

Book Thirteen in a series of twenty-one

With special thanks to Msgr. Francis J. Weber, Archivist of the Los Angeles Catholic Diocese for his encouragement and expertise in developing this series.

This series is dedicated to my sister, Nancy Null Kenyon, whose editing skills and support were so freely given.

Library of Congress Catalog Card Number: 89-90967

ISBN: 1-877599-12-3

Copyright © 1988, Merryant Publishing, 7615 S.W. 257th St., Vashon, WA 98070. No part of this book may be reproduced without permission in writing from the publisher.

Father Junípero Serra

INTRODUCTION

Native American hats were often made of feathers

Building of a mission church involved everyone in the mission community. Priests were engineers and architects; Native Americans did the construction. Mission Indian in front is pouring adobe mix into a brick form. Bricks were then dried in the sun.

FATHER SERRA AND THE MISSIONS: AN INTRODUCTION

The year was 1769. On the east coast of what would soon become the United States, the thirteen original colonies were making ready to break away from England. On the west coast of our continent, however, there could be found only untamed land inhabited by Native Americans, or Indians. Although European explorers had sailed up and down the coast in their ships, no one but American Indians had explored the length of this land on foot . . . until now.

To this wild, beautiful country came a group of adventurous men from New Spain, as Mexico was then called. They were following the orders of their king, King Charles III of Spain.

One of the men was a Spanish missionary named Fray Junípero Serra. He had been given a tremendous job; especially since he was fifty-six years old, an old man in those days. King Charles III had ordered mission settlements to be built along the coast of Alta (Upper) California and it was Fr. Serra's task to carry out the king's wishes.

Father Serra had been born in the tiny village of Petra

on the island of Mallorca, Spain. He had done such an excellent job of teaching and working with the Indians in Mexican missions, the governor of New Spain had suggested to the king that Fr. Serra do the same with the Indians of Alta California. Hard-working Fray Serra was helped by Don Gaspár de Portolá, newly chosen governor of Alta California, and two other Franciscan priests who had grown up with Fr. Serra in Mallorca, Father Fermin Lasuén and Father Francisco Palóu.

There were several reasons why men had been told to build settlements along the coast of this unexplored country. First, missions would help keep the land as Spanish territory. Spain wanted to be sure the rest of the world knew it owned this rich land. Second, missions were to be built near harbors so towns would grow there. Ships from other countries could then stop to trade with the Spaniards, but these travelers could not try to claim the land for themselves. Third, missions were a good way to turn Indians into Christian, hard-working people.

It would be nice if we could write here that everything went well; that twenty-one missions immediately sprang up along the coast. Unfortunately, all did not go well. It would take fifty-four years to build all the California missions. During those fifty-four years many people died from Indian attacks, sickness, and starvation. Earthquakes and fires constantly ruined mission buildings, which then had to be built all over again. Fr. Serra calmly overcame each problem as it happened, as did those priests who followed him.

When a weary Fray Serra finally died in 1784, he had founded nine missions from San Diego to Monterey and had arranged the building of many more. Fr. Lasuén continued Fr. Serra's work, adding eight more missions to the California mission chain. The remaining four missions were founded in later years.

Originally, plans had been to place missions a hard day's walk from each other. Many of them were really quite far apart. Travelers truly struggled to go from one mission to another along the 650 miles of walking road known as El Camino Real, The Royal Highway. Today keen eyes will sometimes see tall, curved poles with bells hanging from them sitting by the side of streets and highways. These bell poles are marking a part of the old El Camino Real.

At first Spanish soldiers were put in charge of the towns which grew up near each mission. The priests were told to handle only the mission and its properties. It did not take long to realize the soldiers were not kind and gentle leaders. Many were uneducated and did not have the understanding they should have had in dealing with people. So the padres came to be in charge of not only the mission, but of the townspeople and even of the soldiers.

The first missions at San Diego and Monterey were built near the ocean where ships could bring them needed supplies. After early missions began to grow their own food and care for themselves, later mission compounds were built farther away from the coast. What one mission did well, such as leatherworking, candlemaking, or raising cattle, was shared with other missions. As a result, missions became somewhat specialized in certain products.

Although mission buildings looked different from mission to mission, most were built from one basic plan. Usually a compound was constructed as a large, four-sided building with an inner patio in the center. The outside of the quadrangle had only one or two doors, which were locked at night to protect the mission. A church usually sat at one corner of the quadrangle and was always the tallest and largest part of the mission compound.

Facing the inner patio were rooms for the two priests living there, workshops, a kitchen. storage rooms for grain and food, and the mission office. Rooms along the back of the quadrangle often served as home to the unmarried Indian women who worked in the kitchen. The rest of the Indians lived just outside the walls of the mission in their own village.

Beyond the mission wall and next to the church was a cemetery. Today you can still see many of the original headstones of those who died while living and working at the mission. Also outside the walls were larger workshops, a reservoir holding water used at the mission, and orchards containing fruit trees. Huge fields surrounded each mission where crops grew and livestock such as sheep, cattle, and horses grazed.

It took a great deal of time for some Indian tribes to understand the new way of life a mission offered, even though the

Native Americans always had food and shelter when they became mission Indians. Each morning all Indians were awakened at sunrise by a church bell calling them to church. Breakfast followed church . . . and then work. The women spun thread and made clothes, as well as cooked meals. Men and older boys worked in workshops or fields and constructed buildings. Meanwhile the Indian children went to school, where the padres taught them. After a noon meal there was a two hour rest before work began again. After dinner the Indians sang, played, or danced. This way of life was an enormous change from the less organized Indian life before the missionaries arrived. Many tribes accepted the change, some had more trouble getting used to a regular schedule, some tribes never became a part of mission life.

Water was all-important to the missions. It was needed to irrigate crops and to provide for the mission people and animals. Priests designed and engineered magnificent irrigation systems at most of the missions. All building of aqueducts and reservoirs of these systems was done by the mission Indians.

With all the organized hard work, the missions did very well. They grew and became strong. Excellent vineyards gave wine for the priests to use and to sell. Mission fields produced large grain crops of wheat and corn, and vast grazing land developed huge herds of cattle and sheep. Mission life was successful for over fifty years.

When Mexico broke away from Spain, it found it did not have enough money to support the California missions, as Spain had been doing. So in 1834, Mexico enforced the secularization law which their government had decreed several years earlier. This law stated missions were to be taken away from the missionaries and given to the Indians. The law said that if an Indian did not want the land or buildings, the property was to be sold to anyone who wished to buy it.

It is true the missions had become quite large and powerful. And as shocked as the padres were to learn of the secularization law, they also knew the missions had originally been planned as temporary, or short term projects. The priests had been sure their Indians would be well-trained enough to run the missions by themselves when the time came to move to other unsettled lands. In fact, however, even after fifty years the California Indians were still not ready to handle the huge missions.

Since the Indians did not wish to continue the missions, the buildings and land were sold, the Indians not even waiting for money or, in some cases, receiving money for the sale.

Sad times lay ahead. Many Indians went back to the old way of life. Some Indians stayed on as servants to the new owners and often these owners were not good to them. Mission buildings were used for everything from stores and saloons to animal barns. In one mission the church became a barracks for the army. A balcony was built for soldiers with their horses stabled in the altar area. Rats ate the stored grain and beautiful church robes. Furniture and objects left by the padres were stolen. People even stole the mission building roof tiles, which then caused the adobe brick walls to melt from rain. Earthquakes finished off many buildings.

Shortly after California became a part of the United States in the mid-1850s, our government returned all mission buildings to the Catholic Church. By this time most of them were in terrible condition. Since the priests needed only the church itself and a few rooms to live in, the other rooms of the mission were rented to anyone who needed them. Strange uses were found in some cases. In the San Fernando Mission, for example, there was once a pig farm in the patio area.

Tourists finally began to notice the mission ruins in the early 1900s. Groups of interested people got together to see if the missions could be restored. Some missions had been "modernized" by this time, unfortunately, but within the last thirty years historians have found enough pictures, drawings, and written descriptions to rebuild or restore most of the missions to their original appearances.

The restoration of all twenty-one missions is a splendid way to preserve our California heritage. It is the hope of many Californians that this dream of restoration can become a reality in the near future.

Original bell of 1794 was sent to mission from Mexico.

MISSION NUESTRA SEÑORA de LA SOLEDAD

I. THE MISSION TODAY

Mission Nuestra Senora de la Soledad means Our Lady of Solitude. It is a most appropriate name. For the mission sits atop a lonely, wind-blown raise of land outside the town of Soledad, overlooking miles of fields and distant mountains. Father Crespi complained of the constant wind many long years ago. He felt the Indians coming to the mission had "been blown in by the four winds". The only true green anywhere seems to be at the mission itself. Here colorful, well-tended gardens and green shrubs brighten the front of the small cloister, or padre's wing.

The mission is in the process of being restored and now consists of a small, recently rebuilt chapel and a seven-room Padre's wing which has a small museum and a gift shop in it.

The chapel walls are adobe brick reconstructed during the 1950s from the dust of original mission bricks. However the new brick, some 20,000 of them made in the same primitive way the Indians made them, have had a material added to them so they will not crumble as easily as the original bricks. The walls are white, inside and out. A bell hangs from a large beam on the left side of the outside wall, near the chapel entrance. It is the original bell sent to the mission in 1794 from Mexico.

The interior of the chapel has a new look to it, but has been decorated in true mission style. A small altar is at the front. A lovely, large statue of Our Lady of the Sorrows sits in a niche behind the altar, forming a simple reredos. It has been done in colors of red and black. The mission's original Stations of the Cross, some of the few items left from the mission days, are hung on the side walls. The wooden benches come from a local parish church and are old enough to fit in with the style of this replica of old Mission Soledad. The chapel is large enough to seat 75-100 people, but daily mass is not celebrated here, for no priest has lived at the mission since 1835.

These days archeologists from UCLA can be seen at the site of the old quadrangle area behind the cloister. Their searching and digging will give us some more information as to the size of Soledad and what was accomplished here almost two hundred years ago. There are so many questions to be answered, but Mission Soledad is beginning to come alive again.

II. HISTORY OF THE MISSION

In 1769 Captain Gaspár de Portolá and Father Juan Crespí, explorer and priest, once spent a night in the valley where Mission Soledad now sits. The men were on their way north to once again search for Monterey Bay. A story tells of them trying to talk with the curious Indians who approached their camp that night, but both men could only recognize a word that sounded like "soledad". In Spanish soledad means loneliness and the word was so descriptive of the hot, treeless, windy valley where they were, that the area was named Soledad at that very moment.

Twenty-two years later, when Father Fermin Lasuén founded the mission on October 9, 1791, Mission Nuestra Señora de la Soledad was the only proper name to give it. A place like this probably would not have been picked for a mission, but there were almost one hundred miles between Mission San Antonio de Padua to the south and Mission Carmel to the north. This was far too long a trip for priests traveling from one mission to the other, so Mission Soledad was built to help ease their journeys between missions.

How symbolic that Mission Soledad was the thirteenth mission in the chain, because life there was always troubled with disasters, one after the other. Records were not well-kept in the early days of the mission, but it is known that brushwood shelters were built at first and that it was six years before there was even an adobe chapel with a straw roof. Perhaps building went slowly because there were so few Indians at the mission. It was the Indians who did the constructing of missions.

More likely the slow growth could have been due to the fact that priests seldom stayed longer than a year at a time here.

Nearly thirty priests came and went during the 44 years the mission was a working mission. Weather was the main reason priests did not stay long enough to accomplish much. Hot, dry summers and bitterly cold winters were not good for the priests' health. What is more, two of the early priests who came to Soledad were particularly not helpful in giving the mission a good start. These two had been wild college friends and were not known for much serious work or fine leadership. They certainly did not help Mission Soledad become successful.

Finally, in 1803, Father Florencio Ibanez arrived at Soledad. This dedicated priest stayed fifteen years and they were good years for the mission. The crops grew well due to an irrigation system using water from two nearby rivers. Cattle, sheep, and horses numbered in the thousands some years. There were 727 people at the mission in 1805, probably the largest the mission ever grew. Epidemics of diseases like flu and measles killed many Indians to be sure, but some Indians simply ran away. At any rate, the mission was always a small one.

In 1814, the first Spanish governor of California came to visit his friend, Fr. Ibanez. The governor died while visiting and was buried in the old church. Four years later Father Ibanez died and was buried next to Governor Arrillaga. They are the only two buried at Mission Soledad whose graves have been located.

One of the worst problems the mission had to face was flooding. The Salinas and Arroyo Seco rivers were small in the summer, when water was needed for crops, but were devastatingly large in the winter.

The flood of 1824 destroyed the large church where Fr. Ibanez and Governor Arrillaga were buried. It was never rebuilt. In 1828 another flood washed away the chapel built to take the church's place. In 1832 the chapel was once again hit by flood, leaving only ruins.

Living through these disasters of nature was Father Vicente Sarria. He had once been the Father-Presidente of the

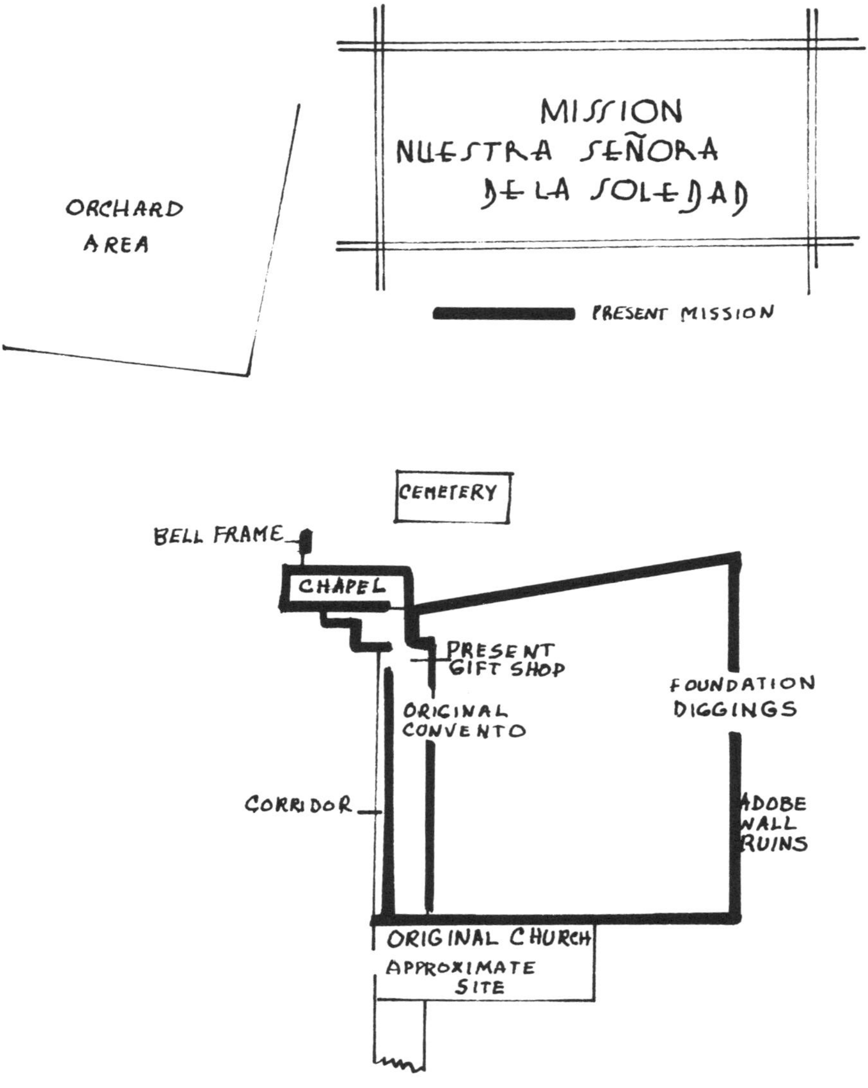

MISSION
NUESTRA SEÑORA
DE LA SOLEDAD
ORCHARD
AREA
PRESENT MISSION
CEMETERY
BELL FRAME
CHAPEL
PRESENT
GIFT SHOP
ORIGINAL
CONVENTO
FOUNDATION
DIGGINGS
CORRIDOR
ADOBE
WALL
RUINS
ORIGINAL CHURCH
APPROXIMATE
SITE

mission chain. He had seen the poor condition of Soledad after Fr. Ibanez's death and felt the Indians needed him. Even after the floods Fr. Sarria continued to take care of the Indians. The mission only grew smaller and poorer, but Fr. Sarria always shared his tiny bit of food with them. Finally, as he was saying mass one day, he fell to the floor. Father Sarria had starved himself to death taking care of his mission Indians. The Indians carried his body all the way to Mission San Antonio de Padua, where he was buried.

Never again was there a priest who lived there. It was a sad ending for a sad and lonely mission. The Mexican secularization law was carried out in 1835, two years later, and Soledad's tile roof was sold to pay off its debt to the Mexican government. The mission was not returned to the Catholic Church until 1859 and without its tile roof, the adobe walls began to dissolve in the weather.

For 90 years the mission sat crumbling in the wind and rain. By 1954, when restoration was begun, only piles of melted adobe dirt were left. The miracle of careful rebuilding can be seen, however, when one visits the Mission Nuestra Señora de la Soledad today. And someday, when the archeologists have finished their research and enough money has been donated for the rebuilding of the mission, one will be able to understand, at last, what an important link Mission Soledad was in the history of the California Missions.

Statue of Our Lady of the Sorrows which sits in a niche above the altar in restored chapel. It is clothed in black lace.

OUTLINE OF MISSION NUESTRA SEÑORA de LA SOLEDAD

I. The mission today

A. Location
   1. Description of location
B. Restoration since 1950s
C. Chapel exterior
   1. Rebuilt
   2. New adobe bricks, original dirt
   3. Color of walls
   4. Bell
      a. Original
      b. Hanging from beam
D. Chapel interior
   1. Altar
   2. Statue of Our Lady of Sorrows
   3. Stations of the Cross
      a. Original
   4. Archeologists

II. History of the mission

A. Naming of the valley in 1769
   1. Capt. Portolá and Fr. Crespí's campsite
B. Founding and naming of mission, October 9, 1791
   1. Fr. Fermin Lasuén
   2. Reason for founding mission
C. Early beginnings
   1. Problems
      a. Weather
      b. Priests
D. Father Ibanez stays fifteen years
   1. Mission grows
      a. Irrigation system
      b. Most Indians in 1805
E. Father Sarria's years
   1. Floods
      a. Loss of big church
      b. Chapel ruined twice
   2. His death from hunger
F. Restoration in 1950s
   1. Archeologists will help write history of mission

GLOSSARY

BUTTRESS: a large mass of stone or wood used to strengthen buildings

CAMPANARIO: a wall which holds bells

CLOISTER: an enclosed area; a word often used instead of convento

CONVENTO: mission building where priests lived

CORRIDOR: covered, outside hallway found at most missions

EL CAMINO REAL: highway between missions; also known as The King's Highway

FACADE: front wall of a building

FONT: large, often decorated bowl containing Holy Water for baptizing people

FOUNDATION: base of a building, part of which is below the ground

FRESCO: designs painted directly on walls or ceilings

LEGEND: a story coming from the past

PORTICO: porch or covered outside hallway

PRESERVE: to keep in good condition without change

PRESIDIO: a settlement of military men

QUADRANGLE: four-sided shape; the shape of most missions

RANCHOS: large ranches often many miles from mission proper where crops were grown and animal herds grazed

REBUILD: to build again; to repair a great deal of something

REPLICA: a close copy of the original

REREDOS: the wall behind the main altar inside the church

***RESTORATION:** to bring something back to its original condition (see * below)

SANCTUARY: area inside, at the front of the church where the main altar is found

SECULARIZATION: something not religious; a law in mission days taking the mission buildings away from the church and placing them under government rule

***ORIGINAL:** the first one; the first one built

BIBLIOGRAPHY

Bauer, Helen. *California Mission Days*. Sacramento, CA: California State Department of Education, 1957.

Goodman, Marian. *Missions of California*. Redwood City, CA: Redwood City Tribune, 1962.

Sunset Editors. *The California Missions*. Menlo Park, CA: Lane Publishing Company, 1979.

Wright, Ralph B., ed. *California Missions*. Arroyo Grande, CA 93420: Hubert A. Lowman, 1977.

For more information about this mission, write to:

Nuestra Señora de la Soledad
Rt. 1 Box 72
Soledad, CA 93960

It is best to enclose a self-addressed, stamped envelope and a small amount of money to pay for brochures and pictures the mission might send you.

Acknowledgement
Nora Campbell, Manager, Gift Shop

CREDITS

Cover art and Father Serra Illustration: Ellen Grim
Illustrations: Alfredo de Batuc
Ground Layout: Mary Boulé
Printing: Pollard Group, Inc.